HURRICANE HUMANS

Abhijit Naskar is the twenty-first century Neuroscientist whose contributions in Cognitive and Behavioral Neuroscience have helped the world tackle the issues of mental illness, prejudice, hate, extremism, discrimination and segregation more effectively. As an untiring advocate of mental health and universal acceptance, he became a beloved best-selling author all over the world with his very first book "The Art of Neuroscience in Everything". With his pioneering ventures into the Neuropsychology of beliefs and biases, he has hugely contributed in the eradication of religious and cultural differences in our world, for which he is popularly hailed as a humanitarian scientist, who takes the human civilization in the path of sweet general harmony.

HURRICANE HUMANS

GIVE ME ACCOUNTABILITY,
I'LL GIVE YOU PEACE

ABHIJIT NASKAR

Hurricane Humans:

Give Me Accountability, I'll Give You Peace

Copyright © 2020 Abhijit Naskar

This is a work of non-fiction

An Amazon Publishing Company, 1st Edition, 2020

Printed in the United States of America

ISBN: 9798670557849

Also by Abhijit Naskar

The Art of Neuroscience in Everything
Your Own Neuron: A Tour of Your Psychic Brain
The God Parasite: Revelation of Neuroscience
The Spirituality Engine
Love Sutra: The Neuroscientific Manual of Love
Homo: A Brief History of Consciousness
Neurosutra: The Abhijit Naskar Collection
Autobiography of God: Biopsy of A Cognitive Reality
Biopsy of Religions: Neuroanalysis towards Universal
Tolerance
Prescription: Treating India's Soul
What is Mind?
In Search of Divinity: Journey to The Kingdom of Conscience
Love, God & Neurons: Memoir of a scientist who found
himself by getting lost
The Islamophobic Civilization: Voyage of Acceptance
Neurons of Jesus: Mind of A Teacher, Spouse & Thinker
Neurons, Oxygen & Nanak
The Education Decree
Principia Humanitas
The Krishna Cancer
Rowdy Buddha: The First Sapiens
We Are All Black: A Treatise on Racism
The Bengal Tigress: A Treatise on Gender Equality
Either Civilized or Phobic: A Treatise on Homosexuality
Wise Mating: A Treatise on Monogamy
Illusion of Religion: A Treatise on Religious
Fundamentalism
The Film Testament
Human Making is Our Mission: A Treatise on Parenting
I Am The Thread: My Mission
7 Billion Gods: Humans Above All
Lord is My Sheep: Gospel of Human
Morality Absolute
A Push in Perception
Let The Poor Be Your God
Conscience over Nonsense
Saint of The Sapiens
Time to Save Medicine
Fabric of Humanity

Build Bridges not Walls: In the name of Americana
The Constitution of The United Peoples of Earth
Lives to Serve Before I Sleep
When Humans Unite: Making A World Without Borders
All For Acceptance
Monk Meets World
Mission Reality
Citizens of Peace: Beyond The Savagery of Sovereignty
Operation Justice: To Make A Society That Needs No Law
See No Gender
The Gospel of Technology
Every Generation Needs Caretakers: The Gospel of
Patriotism
Aşkanjali: The Sufi Sermon
Mad About Humans: World Maker's Almanac
Revolution Indomable
When Call The People: My World My Responsibility
No Foreigner Only Family

DEDICATION

Patrick Henry and Thomas Paine

CONTENTS

1. In Line of Service
(The Sonnet)

In Line of Service
(The Sonnet)

World is my Louisiana,
I am its Mississippi.
Whenever it's in trouble,
My blood boils in agony.
Each drop of tear around,
Makes my bones ignite.
My life finds its meaning,
As I respond to their plight.
Joy is only joy to me,
When I bring it to others.
If gained in line of service,
Even wounds are my treasures.
Once I die for the people's future,
Then I can live in peace forever.

2. Price of Harmony

Civilization starts with freedom and accountability. We'll get to the accountability part later on. First let's talk about freedom, that is, liberation or emancipation or self-determination. Freedom demands blood - are you ready to bleed - are you ready to turn into ashes - are you ready to burn in a thousand fires of hell - if you are, only then can the people have actual practical emancipation - only then can the people have true equality - only then can there be actual harmony on this planet.

So, be ready - be prepared - be absolutely upfront with your head held high and your body extended at utmost will in sacrifice. You think harmony is a theory that you just read in some ragged books and that's it, the world magically receives all the harmony it needs - it doesn't work like that.

Harmony and peace can never manifest so long as they remain theories - so long as they remain ideas to be taught and debated over - so long as they remain bound by heavy words on the pages of books. Rise above the books and taste the harmony that flows through your veins - rise above the books and unleash the peace that is dying to break out from your nerve endings into the world outside.

It all starts with you - with you the being of flesh and blood - with you the being of conscience and character - with you the being of upfront and forthright righteousness - no theories, no philosophies, no ceremonies, all that the world needs is your unbound determination and unbending dignity in the course of assimilation.

Be the revolutionary of your time, for every time is human time and human time is born of human mind, which itself is a fusion of good and bad. Hence, to treat the bad and empower the good, every time needs its revolutionary - and that revolutionary is you - the person born of nature - the person who makes mistakes - the person who fails - the person who feels sad, miserable and even desperate at times - but that person never stops - that person never ceases action - that person never stays a failure for long - that person never dwells in the mistakes - that person is the very manifestation of progress - all progress starts from that person - from that individual - all progress starts from you - you, who is a human - an ordinary, everyday, regular human with regular feelings of joy and sorrow.

When the need arises that ordinary you has the force of the universe inside to turn you into the indomitable lifeforce of desolation - yes you heard right - you must turn into the indomitable lifeforce of desolation - desolating bigotry - desolating injustice - desolating discrimination and prejudice.

Nonviolence doesn't mean silence, nonviolence means action out of conscience. And when the world is in pain, all that you should be bothered with is that pain - all that should be in your mind is to alleviate that pain - all that should be in front of your eyes is the wailing faces of the people in pain - of your people - of our people. Seeing all this if you remain silent in the name of nonviolence or in the name of practicality, or in the name of security, then all I can say is, shame on you - shame on you as a human - shame on you as a being of conscience - shame on you as a being of character - shame on your very life. What are you good for, if your life doesn't make a single trace of contribution in the alleviation of people's misery!

A thousand church visits won't make you holy, if you remain indifferent to the agonies of the people. Bring out the spirit of the church from inside you and turn into the living force of divinity, by lending a hand to those in need. It's not kindness - it's not charity - it's not selflessness - it's just plain ordinary humanity.

Forget the philosophies, forget the gospels, forget the preachings, dogmas and doctrines, forget all the theories that attempt to teach you how to be divine or how to be intellectual, or how to be holy - just be a plain ordinary human who helps another human, and that's all there is to becoming the practical embodiment of divinity - to becoming the practical symposium of all the enlightenment in the world - to becoming the supreme force of actual living holiness.

What is holy, what is not, can't be determined by rituals and ceremonies, it can only be determined by human action, for every act of humaneness is holiness itself. And humaneness doesn't just mean lifting the poor and the destitute, it also means defending the weak - it means standing on guard against brutality to defend the helpless - it means becoming a shield to the discriminated and oppressed and a sword to discrimination and oppression.

In an interview I was asked, will it be easy for an individual to stand up to the discrimination and oppression in the society? And my answer was - easy, no - necessary, yes - because the alternative is way worse. It's worthless to be hopeful for the future, if there is no action on your part. It's not about hope or faith, it's about the basic accountability of the ordinary human to stand up to inhumanity.

Remember, O Mighty Soldiers, destiny has no power over you, for you are the mothers and fathers of destiny. Destiny is born of your actions - it's born of your own two hands - it's born of your footsteps. Where there are footsteps, there is destiny - no footsteps, no destiny. Wipe out all concepts, myths, traditions and theories of destiny from your mind, and forge your destiny yourself - and your destiny will carve the destiny of your society.

3. Society over Separatism

If your culture creates a barrier between you and society, then break all ties with such culture - if your traditions create a barrier between you and society, then break all ties with such traditions - if your religion creates a barrier between you and society, then break all allegiance to such religion - if your intellect creates a barrier between you and society, then destroy your reliance on such egotistic intellect.

Anything that creates a separation between the self and society must be discarded from life at once. Nothing - I repeat, noting is more important that your belonging to humanity - not culture, not traditions, not religion, not messiahs, prophets and gods, not intellect, nothing. Humanity first, then everything else, or else, one might as well be living in the jungle where one belongs.

You know why peace is still a concept and not a reality? It's because we are all cooped up in little cocoons and think of our own cocoon to be superior to all others. The philosopher thinks their philosophy is the best, the preacher thinks their religion is the best, the scientist thinks their science is the best, and so on. The existential fact of the matter is, none of it is superior to others.

Each of them has their role to play, and that role is to serve the people.

To put it simply, philosophy is not more important than the people - religion is not more important than the people - science is not more important than the people. And whenever they start taking the people for granted and begin thinking of themselves to be all-important, they set off on a road to doom and destruction, both for themselves and the world.

4. Allegiance to Humanity

The wise recognizes and embraces the roles of all the threads of the societal fabric, whereas the shallow swears their allegiance to one thread and sees all others as enemies. If there is one force that is worthy of the allegiance of humans, it is the force of humanity - and once you do, you would automatically begin to recognize the potential in all the threads of the society. I am a scientist, but my allegiance (not to be taken as obedience, but as commitment) is not to science, it is to humanity - I don't serve science, science is only a tool in my service to humanity.

Likewise, a preacher who swears allegiance to humanity, never serves religion, instead uses religion as a tool to serve humanity. A philosopher who swears allegiance to humanity, never serves philosophy, instead uses philosophy as a tool to serve humanity. The same goes for every single person on earth - every single human that is.

One who is committed to humanity, never serves culture, tradition, religion or intellect - these are all secondary, to those who have realized the value of humanity, hence compromisable. But nothing can make them compromise their commitment to humanity.

They would rather die than compromise humanity.

The world is my home and all humans are my kith and kin - thus speaks the human - thus feels the being of conscience and character. Does this mean that there won't be any religion, nation or cultural traditions in the world? In an ideal world, there indeed won't be any such thing - but ours in not an ideal world, and it doesn't need to be. All that is needed is that we break our ties to such sectarianism - once we have successfully done that, then we could not only celebrate all the traditions, but more importantly we could all celebrate them together with no concern for which religion, nation or culture they come from.

Borders on the maps are not the problem, borders in our heart are. Once we erase those borders at our own free will, borders of the world will merely remain as technical specifications of a functional global society, and not as walls of separation between people. How dare some ragged norms separate people on the basis of geography - how dare some ragged traditions separate people on the basis of books of the dead - how dare some modern norms separate people on the basis of intellect, profession and stature!

Separation is bondage, oneness is liberation. Segregation is degradation, assimilation is ascension. And worse than segregation is glorifying that segregation as tradition, be it religious, national or intellectual - it is the very opposite of holiness - it is the very opposite of civilization - it is the very opposite of progress. All separation goes against humanity, and anything that goes against humanity goes against progress.

Of course there will be impediments - of course there will be obstructions - no great purpose is every achieved without obstruction. The more the obstructions the greater your impact. Sleep not, slacken not and work - work the idea, throw the self overboard and work for the masses - work for the poorest and lowliest - elevation of the masses without injuring their individuality - keep this motto in front of you. Work, work and work elevating the masses and you will conquer the whole world with your love.

Work for the people - work for the society, but join no sect or cult. Say to yourself - what have I to do with this "ism" and that "ism" - I am the servant of humanity, and as such I work with every ism, but will never join any of them. Above all isms humanity must be engraved in our heart and practiced every day to the letter and spirit, that is, we must stand ready to defend its honor, sanity and serenity at all cost, without submitting to the age-old practice of indifference.

5. Indifference is not Nonviolence

Differences don't make a society fall, indifference does. Rise and fall of a society are predicated on human action, or in case of the latter, it's inaction. But here is the interesting part, many have confused inaction to be the path of nonviolence. To understand nonviolence we must understand in our heart what violence means. And here I am not talking about bookish definitions - I am not talking about more theories - I am not talking about ideologies of the dead, religious or otherwise. With changing times every idea must evolve, if it doesn't then it causes more harm than good in the hands of its devout believers.

So, let's understand violence and nonviolence shall we! I am a devout believer in nonviolence, but if someone harms another person in front of me, then standing up to such savagery is basic humanity, and if an act of basic humanity goes against ideas of the past, then it is those ideas that should be questioned, not our humanity.

Now the question that rises is, should we get rid of the idea of nonviolence altogether? The idea of nonviolence is not as black and white as traditional opinions have made the world believe. It's all quite grey. And while investigating the grey areas of the society, we must tread cautiously.

Nonviolence is not the same as indifference. Accepting violence is not nonviolence, it is also violence. So, what is nonviolence one wonders! Nonviolence is an everyday trait of the mind that keeps you from fostering hate against others - that keeps you from acting out of hate.

So, now we must ask the most important question. If nonviolence is an active trait of one's mind, what happens when one is faced with violence, whether on the self or on others! Don't wait for me to answer the question, instead place yourself in such a situation in your mind and ask yourself what would you do?

Forget nonviolence, forget Naskar, forget Christ - forget all the philosophies in the world - simply ask yourself as a regular human with no knowledge of sophisticated philosophical notions. Imagine someone is trying to harm your sibling or partner or parent or friend - what would you do? It's this simple. Would you stand back and say nothing - do nothing? Or would you stand up - speak up - and defend your loved ones, not out of hate, but simply out of care - out of responsibility? Any breathing and living human would choose the latter over the former. And that is real, practical nonviolence - that is right human action - an action born not of hate but of responsibility.

To clear this matter further let me put it this way - the only way to know whether an act is nonviolent or not, is by asking whether that act is born of hate or responsibility. And in this fundamental act of responsibility - in this fundamental act of conscience, lies the seed of a warfree planet.

6. Building A World without War

We can end all wars on earth only when the individuals of conscience learn to stand up to the everyday inhumanities in their corners of society. When the regular humans start to think for themselves and act out of conscience and not impulse, only then will the greed and savageries of a few bugs within the state and other domains of the society turn absolutely powerless to turn people against people. So, if you learn to think - if you learn to question, first your own nation, then other nations - first your own actions, then those of others, will we witness the rise of true practical peace for the first time in the history of life on earth.

To build a warfree society, each of us must work to build a warfree self, and the only way to do that is to disavow allegiance to anything that separates the self from the society. Disavow your culture if needed - disavow your religion if needed - disavow your nation if needed - disavow anything and everything that teaches you self-obsession and narcissism – and never let any traditional construct undermine your humanity. If you can do that, then your neighborhood will have at least one living breathing flame of oneness and that flame will light up the untamable fire of peace in many more.

Peace doesn't mean lack of violence, but the presence of conscience to stand up to violence. As I have said in "No Foreigner Only Family", *strength used for oppression is violence, strength used for defending the weak is justice."* So, do not be a blind stickler to the popular, unscrutinized concept of nonviolence, and wake up the basic everyday responsibility in your nerves to step beyond mass hysteria. Strictly obeying a concept without thinking about whether it's compatible with the needs of the new time and age, takes civilization backwards not forwards.

Let me give you an example. Let's talk about the most popular figure of nonviolence – Gandhi. If it wasn't for Gandhi-led Indian National Congress' orthodox obsession of the theoretical concept of nonviolence, the country called India would've gained independence from British oppression much earlier than 1947. In India the nonviolent movement led by Gandhi had a very different face than the nonviolent movement in America led by Gandhi's most revered pupil MLK.

Gandhi-inspired MLK's nonviolent movement along with the enthusiastic efforts of not so non-violent patriots like Malcolm X and others turned out to be a grand success, whereas Gandhi's nonviolent movement in his own country made very little contribution to the liberation of India.

However, do not assume that I am undermining Gandhi in any manner. In fact, I have learnt a great many things from him. But what I am pointing out is the real life implications of Gandhi's action in the liberation movement of his own country. He is indeed one of the greatest and gentlest minds of our world, but he showed his gentleness in a situation where it only facilitated the oppression of the tyrants. That is why, he was the least qualified person to be dubbed the father of India.

The only reason Gandhi is seen as the father of India is because the first political party that gained power after the independence of India was led by Gandhi himself. Naturally Gandhi became the figurehead of the nation and his main wingman Jawaharlal Nehru became the first prime minister of free India (India is a

Prime Minister run nation, unlike our states which is a President run nation).

The fact of the matter is, there were hundreds of actual patriots who were more qualified for the title of the father of India than Gandhi. And at the very top of the list we could place only one person – Bose (not the physicist). The true father of free India was Subhas Chandra Bose, not Gandhi. Bose loved and admired Gandhi greatly, but didn't accept Gandhi's notion that nonviolence was the path to India's Independence from the British - and quite rightly so.

To put this into perspective - imagine Commander Washington asking his troops to never fire back a single musket ball no matter how many british guns are fired at them. And that's exactly what Gandhi asked of his people. Bose eventually raised the Indian National Army to fight against the British in India. Subhas Chandra Bose is to India what George Washington is to the United States of America. Unfortunately, Bose lost his life in a plane crash in 1945, but had he lived, he would've been the rightful prime minister of India, not Jawaharlal

Nehru, who was more of a scholar, than a leader.

However, the death of Bose and the struggles of the Indian National Army lighted the fire of revolution in the heart of the entire nation empowering them to revolt against the mighty British Empire, which compelled the British to leave all imperialist authority over India in the year 1947.

Here is a simple fact of the matter - oppressors do not understand the language of the traditional concept of nonviolence. It took blood of the common everyday Americans to free our land of liberty from the clutches of British authority and the same is true for India. It took blood of the Indians to free the ancient land of spirituality from the clutches of British imperialism. In fact, it is the common history of every single oppressed nation.

No unfree country has ever been freed through indifference. Liberty demands sacrifice - liberty demands revolution. Let me give you an example. If America stands today as a free country, it's because of those Americans who sacrificed their lives fighting against the redcoats. But there is another side of American history which is not taught in schools. And it's the bitter side of the story, so brace for it.

The only reason the country called America even exists is because the native americans who were living in the land for a long time before the pilgrims arrived here from Europe, couldn't organize a large and strong enough uprising to fight them away from their land. This is more reason for each person of this sweet land of liberty to practice assimilation not segregation - this is more reason for each of us to come to the aid of the oppressed and segregated - this is more reason for each of us to stand upright against discrimination, narcissism, prejudice and sectarianism.

The existential reality of an organic, amateur and decently intelligent species like ours is that turning the other cheek to an oppressor will leave you and your loved ones without a head, so foster peace in mind, but at the same time foster the courage to stand up to oppression. Don't stick to any one concept, old or new, to such an extent that you lose touch with practical life. A concept, no matter how old or new, if doesn't serve everyday practical living, then it's worthless.

Accepting violence is not nonviolence, it's violence itself. So, foster thought, foster conscience, foster responsibility - think, think and think - then act out of your thought, act out of your conscience, act out of your responsibility and forget everything else.

7. Character is Foundation

Fill your mind with one pure, uncorrupted, indivisible, sanctimonious force - the force of community - push it to every corner of your being - and then broadcast it into the world through your actions. Community is the window to a world without war - a world absolutely loved, absolutely trusted - a world beyond strategies, beyond segregation, beyond separatism - a world of pure, unbending, unravaged universalism - can you see that world my friend - do you perceive a glimpse of that world - right now - right this moment, for a glimpse is all you need - a glimpse of liberty - a glimpse of nonrigidility - a glimpse of wholeness born of nothingness - from perception rises realization - from realization rises action - and in action will the world without war be born.

It is this simple - if your society lacks a bridge, be the bridge - if your society lacks voice, be the voice - if your society lacks courage, be the courage - if your society lacks conscience, be the conscience. Fill in for the weaknesses of your society. And when each corner of the world has a handful of such bravehearts to fill in for the weaknesses of their society, no separatism will have the power to survive for long. Give me hundred bravehearts with character, I'll give you a world without war.

Building a world without war is easy, once a handful of humans have built themselves. Build the human in you - build its conscience - build its righteousness - build its character. Remember, a cup of character will go a longer way than barrels of instincts (in the biological sense of the term, that is, basic instinctual drives, such as libido, hunger, belief and so on).

Let's go very slow here, for the matter of instincts is rather grey area. However, when you take human evolution in consideration, that greyness slowly becomes quite black and white, at least in case of instincts. The purpose of instincts is survival, nothing more - a mechanism born of life in the wild. So, if you rely on your instincts, you may succeed in surviving, but that survival has no relation whatsoever to building a life in a civilized manner - hence, it has no relation whatsoever to building a civilized society - a society of conscience - a society of character.

To build a society of character you must first build your own character. Better lose life than character. Work on your character every single day, for your character is to be the foundation stone of your society. You my friend, are the foundation stone of your society. You are the rock to your society. But mark you, this doesn't necessarily mean that you have to give up life as it is - all you have to do is lend a hand to those in need around you - all you need to do is feel responsible of your community.

One who feels responsible for their community, needs no ancestor to define their identity. Your identity lies in your action, not in your ancestry. If you do good, that goodness becomes your identity - if you help a stranger, that help becomes your identity - if you accept all people as your own kith and kin, that acceptance becomes your identity.

It's your action that makes you immortal, not your ancestry. Your power is in your determination, not in your pedigree. Don't rely on your heritage, become your own heritage. Fight, fight, fight my warriors - fight for the alive future, not for a dead past. Here I am not implying that you should forget your past - in fact, you must never forget your past, but you must not cling to your past to such an extent that you lose sight of the present.

We are who we are because of our past and we will be who we will be because of our present. So take control of your present and your future is secured. But by control I am not talking about a mechanical, harsh control of your life, rather I am talking about a basic, everyday, gentle grip over your actions. Act and you shall receive. Action begets destiny.

Rise above your past - rise above heritage - rise above tradition and build a world where the humans value humans above everything else. I am human by birth, human by heart and human by action, I don't need any other shallow identity. Geography is for the savages to fight over - religion is for the savages to fight over - intellect is for the savages to fight over - I am but a human, above and beyond the petty squabbles of societal labels. Religion is futile to me - culture is futile to me - nationality is futile to me - everything is futile to me, except humanity. Humans above all else, that's the motto for a civilized human.

8. One Species, One Anthem, One Motto

Civilization and being civilized are two different things - the former refers to a species smart enough to build a kingdom of their own separate from the wild, technically speaking that is, whereas the latter refers to the character of that species. So, now the question is, are you civilized - are we civilized? Wearing fancy clothes and speaking fluent english don't make you civilized, what does is your behavior with others.

How do you behave with others - how do you behave with a person getting out of a limousine wearing a fancy suit and how do you behave with a janitor - think in your head - is there a difference between the two behaviors - no need to hide or pretend, for nobody is judging you here, it's just you and me - and my purpose is not to judge you, but to make you think - so think, do you behave the same with a janitor as you behave with a fancy suit person! If not, why! What makes one person more important than the other! Remember, until the billionaire and the janitor become equal in your eyes, you are yet to be a civilized human. It's this simple. It has nothing to do with your faith - it has nothing to do with your riches - it has nothing to do with your intellect.

Being civilized requires being human and being human requires valuing a human above the societal labels, no matter how dear some of those labels are to you. Hold labels dear, wars will prevail - hold people dear, wars will disappear. People like to believe that politicians are responsible for the wars on this planet, but the fact of the matter is, it's the people who are responsible for each and every war - my nation is the best, my religion is the best, my language is the best, my culture is the best - this way of thinking has ripped this world into pieces and then when some greedy politicians, bureaucrats and billionaires play politics with those pieces, people throw all blame on them for the conflicts on earth. What a damned hypocrisy!

You know what's wrong with this world - everyone says it's not their fault, but guess what – it is - all of it - it's all your fault - it's all our fault. So, what are you going to do about it! Are you going to keep blaming each other - or are you for once take responsibility! If the world is at war, it's our fault - if the world is in conflict, it's our fault - if the world is in peril, it's our fault. We can whine and blame all we want like little kids, but that's not going to change anything. So, we must take charge - you must take charge - take charge of your neighborhood - take charge of your society - take charge of your world - of our world.

Remember this golden principle, one species, one anthem, one motto - assimilation. Realization of community is the beginning of assimilation. That's all there is to it, that is, community - society. But mark you, here I am not talking about community defined by labels, I am talking about community of people. It's this simple - wherever you are, the people around become your community, including those who arrive later from other lands. It's not the geography that makes the community, it's the community that makes the geography.

So, be one with your community, be responsible for your community, build your community and assimilate all who come through the gates. Assimilate all, celebrate each other's joy and invigorate each other through weakness. Your wait for the second coming is over, for the savior is already here, it's us, each one of us. Recognize that savior within and unleash it into the world.

9. Peace Sonnet

52

Peace Sonnet

Peace doesn't grow on trees,
Nor is it produced in factories.
It has been a concept of books,
Must it stay that way for centuries!
Where argumentation is afoot,
The mission becomes a phantom.
Where the mind thrives on tradition,
Peace is an inconvenience to the norm.
Peace is but a myth most foul,
An annoying goal that demands a lot.
We just prefer our cozy cocoons,
Giving up any of it is just plain absurd.
But there is a cure to the war disease.
Loosen your knots and there'll be peace.

54

10. Dream Peace,
Think Peace, Live Peace

You don't make peace, you are peace. Peace is alive through you - through your action - you cease action and peace dies with it. It's all in the individual, not the collective, for the collective starts with the individual. Action of an individual is not just action of an individual, it's the action of an entire species. You are not insignificant - your life is not meaningless - you have the power of the universe in your nerves to take this world ahead in a direction of your choice. So, choose wisely.

Peace is a short and simple enough word, but its manifestation and implications are still a myth - mere matter of books - to take it out of the books into the real world you must step beyond the egotistical bounds of your intellectual understanding of peace. Peace is to be lived, not taught or learnt. So, dream peace, think peace, live peace - dream warlessness, think warlessness, live warlessness.

Warlessness doesn't mean lack of conflict or disagreement, it means lack of hate. To put it simply, warlessness means hatelessness. War is not born of conflict, war is born of hate fostered in conflict. Here, some may wonder, aren't war and conflict the same thing! On the surface they may appear to be the same, but if you go deeper while considering their psychological implications, then the real picture will begin to appear.

If we consider that conflict means disagreement, then conflict and war cannot be the same, because in this case if they are, we would never be able to rid this world of wars. Let me tell you why. It's because it is biologically impossible for an intelligent organic species such as ourselves to not have disagreements. So you see, disagreements or conflicts are not the problem, the problem is our instinctual drive to foster a hateful separation with the person we disagree with. Once we step beyond that hate, all wars will automatically disappear, for though we will have our conflicts they won't have hate in them to fuel a war. Hate is the prime fuel for war, destroy the hate and all wars will end.

Let's build this world - let's make a fresh start - let's make it from ground up - and this time let's make it without prejudice - without loyalty - without walls. Let's make this world our way, that is, a world without hate - a world for the humans, by the humans, of the humans, that's it.

Let's forget what our ancestors did or did not do, and let's take things in our own hands. Let's think for ourselves, let's feel for ourselves, let's observe for ourselves and above all let's act for ourselves. So, feel, think and act, based on your own faculties, without the conditioning of culture and society. Be bold, be honest and do you, that's all you need to remember.

Once you can truly start feeling, thinking and acting upon your own faculties, all prejudices will begin to lose their grip over you, and once the prejudices lose their grip, so does hate. And when hate loses its grip over you the individual, eventually it'll lose grip over the world, hence leading to a world without wars.

A lot of time has been wasted by the nations of planet earth on strategies of war, it's time we start organizing peace instead. My very existence is a manifestation of that mission. I am a revolution for united humanity, and till the whole of humankind is united beyond race, religion and ideology, this revolution will continue in one lionheart or another. Just like all the revolutions of human history continue in me.

Not a single revolutionary life of this planet has gone lost - they all live on in me - MLK lives on in me - Mandela lives on in me - Rosa Parks lives on in me - Patrick Henry lives on in me - Subhas Chandra Bose lives on in me - Bhagat Singh lives on in me - my thoughts, ambitions and actions represent their combined thoughts, ambitions and actions - and once my mortal body perishes I too will live on in the next revolutionary, and in the next and in the next. Remember, the supreme dream of us revolutionaries is only one - it's to rid this world of all oppression, discrimination and segregation.

A revolutionary never submits to oppression, they fight till death. Just once let me die for the people, then I can live in peace. Remember, measure life not by years, but by good deeds, not because you'll receive some imaginary "karmic" reward for being good, but because life without goodness is but death in disguise.

11. Sonnet of Culture

Sonnet of Culture

Our culture their culture,
Enough of this primitive nonsense.
It may have suited our ancestors,
But it suits not beings of conscience.
Of all nations on the face of earth,
My nation is the greatest.
This is no behavior of the civilized,
It's but a sign of the stupidest.
The savage jungle or modern society,
What would you like to be a part of?
Your choice means absolutely nothing,
Till you act on the accountability thereof.
Boasting ancestry declares a dead character.
Wake up from death to write a new chapter.

12. Question of Identity

Why are we living? Are we living just so we could breathe - are we living just so we could eat - are we living just so we could wear fancy clothes – are we living just so we could sleep with people - or is there something more to this thing called life! And by something more, I am not talking about all that supernatural, mystical and metaphysical nonsense. Rather I am simply talking about the natural fundamentals of life, not the biological fundamentals mark you, but psychological fundamentals, that is, courage, conscience and compassion. Without these three fundamentals, whether you are biologically alive or not, doesn't really matter, for your life is no different from the life of an animal in the jungle.

We all come from the jungle, but whether we keep that jungle alive or not depends on us. Why not give it a nice burial and move ahead with civilized footsteps! Civilization hangs on a thin thread, the thread of our humanity, that is, the humanity of the individual human – the humanity within each one of us.

Forget the society for the time being and place yourself at the focus of inquiry. Ask yourself, what are you okay with? Are you okay with the world being turned back into the kingdom of the wild by savage recklessness? Or are you going to do something about it? And by doing something, I am not talking about cooking up who to blame, rather I am talking about taking responsibility yourself, for your very humanity is predicated on your responsibility. Without responsibility there is no humanity, but only savagery.

So, living your life conforming to every single norm of your environment doesn't make you a human, nor does rebelling against the norms simply for the sake of being called different. You are human only if you take responsibility for your society - you are human only if you are ready to take a stand against certain norms when the need arises to right the wrong.

You are human when you stand up to your society and announce at the top of your voice - this is wrong. If the humans do not stand up to right the wrongs, soon the world will be overrun by vermin. So, it's not a matter of hoping for a better future, it's a matter of stepping up to make that better future. Future doesn't spring out of hopes and wishes, it requires action.

It's this simple - peace is love, love is peace. However, though this sounds simple enough, in practice, it hardly ever is that simple, primarily because of humankind's innate affinity to manmade identities. Peace does not exist, because humans care more about their identity than peace or even people for that matter. Naturally, peace on earth still remains a concept, and not reality.

Here some may argue that what are we without our identity! And that is indeed a valid point, but it's rather outdated, given the stark globalization of our species. Most of the identities that we hold most dear were invented in a tribal world, where one tribe of people in one corner of the world had no substantial relations to another tribe of people in another corner of the world. Hence tribe was everything to them - and preservation of the tribe was of utmost significance, even if it meant harming and exploiting other tribes.

A bunch of people from one tribe boldly went into the land of another tribe looting, pillaging and raping and they brought back food, clothing and women as souvenirs of victory and they called this valor and patriotism. And the stories of these exploits would be passed on through generations as some sort of heroic saga. And nobody would question it, for questioning those stories would mean questioning the tribal traditions, which would be an act of treason.

Now my question to you, the thinking human of a modern world is - this kind of behavior may have been accepted in those days as uncompromisable tradition when our ancestors were nothing more than mindless savages, but does such tribalism make any sense in a civilized abode such as ours!

Tribalism and civilization cannot exist side by side. You must let go of one to let the other flourish. For example, you simply cannot take pride in the imperialist atrocities of your ancestors and at the same time call yourself a civilized human. You are either an imperialist or human, you cannot be both - you are either a nationalist or human, you cannot be both - you are either tribal or civilized, you cannot be both. Tribalism has no place whatsoever in a civilized society, no matter how much you polish it and stick a new label on top of it. Tribalism causes separation and separation disrupts peace.

So we must understand further, what is tribalism? To put it in simple terms, tribalism is obsessing over the illusive supremacy of one's own tribe over others. You may label it however you like - label it religion, label it nationality, label it ideology - if you are obsessing over the grandeur of your own tribal identity over the others, then you are a tribal, therefore, not a human. Such an act is downright savagery, even if you memorize thousands of books to defend your tribalism.

Humans above all, if you don't understand this simple fact, then your intellect is no better than the intellect of a cannibal. Intellectually you can find arguments in favor of and against every single act in the world, but such arguments mean nothing, as long as their purpose is to defend sectarianism and not people. Hence, intellect is futile if it aids sectarianism instead of humanizing the world.

However, here I must mention that, I am not talking about getting rid of all your cultural identities, for such is neurologically an impossible task, but what I am saying is that, you must not hold on to your own cultural identities so strongly that you start seeing others as enemies. Holding on to your identity is not tribalism, but holding on to the illusive grandeur of that identity is.

All societal identities are illusive. Your parents are not your identity - your ancestors are not your identity - your culture is not your identity - your traditions are not your identity. You have no identity until you make one with your actions. Your action is your identity, there is nothing else.

All the identity that some people have is that they are their parent's children - I pity these people, for if you ask them "who are you without your parents" - their very existence would be wiped out. The same is true for those whose only identity is that they are the descendants of their ancestors. This is not identity, this is delusion. And sustaining such delusion will only lead to a more behaviorally shallow and internally insecure society.

Ask yourself, what is your identity? What are you without your ancestors? What are you without your traditions? What are you without your faith? What are you without your nationality? What are you without your culture?

Don't be cynical or critical, just be inquisitive and ask.

Nothing good ever comes out of cynicism. Only inquisitiveness reveals answers. So, be inquisitive, be curious and all the answers you seek will unfold in front of you. Answers favor the inquisitive. So, be inquisitive about the world - be inquisitive about the self – first the self, then the world, for when you understand yourself better, you'll understand the world better. Because the world outside is but a reflection of the world inside.

Hence, in your identity lies the identity of the world. If you hold on to the narcissistic grandeur of your illusive tribal identities, then the world will keep burning in the everlasting battles among tribes. But if you could loosen the knots of your illusive identities and make a novel identity for yourself with your actions, then all traces of rigidity and tribalism would begin to vanish from the face of earth.

Discover your identity - a novel identity - an identity which is uncorrupt and unconditioned - an identity that exudes who you are, not who your ancestors were - an identity that is neither pure nor impure, but purely you. My identity is my work - my identity is my ideas - my identity is the mission of united humanity. What is your identity?

Don't compare yourself with me or with any other, because comparison is degradation. Find your purpose, work your identity and live with immortality. Immortal are not those who never die, immortal are those who don't hesitate to die for a purpose. The fate of this world is predicated on your purpose - yes, you heard right - the fate of our planet is predicated on your purpose, for your purpose is the force that the world needs to rid itself of its systemic atrocities.

Many people often ask me, can there ever be peace on earth? I tell them, the question is not whether there can be peace on earth, but how far are you willing to go to ensure peace on earth? When people think of peace, they think of it as a concept, so they keep discussing and arguing over it, with zero clarity of the matter. But ask them, what are you going to have for dinner tonight, and they'll give you all sorts of details about it. Because to people dinner is more real, practical and crucial than peace on earth.

The moment peace becomes as real, practical and crucial to the people of earth as dinner, there will be no need for any more messiah to rise and advocate for world peace, for each human being will be an epitome of peace and harmony.

13. Self and Society
(The Sonnet)

Self and Society
(The Sonnet)

I and you are not two but one,
The space in-between is an illusion.
The air you breathe is also in me,
Then why hang on to separation!
Where there is dark ignorance,
There festers delusion most foul.
Once you give in to such atrocity,
Society breaks out in painful howl.
Self and society are one whole being,
That's how we make a humane world.
But if this is none of your concern,
You are but a bug with conscience curled.
Fabric of society is everyone's business.
It's time we breathe life into humaneness.

14. Beyond Self-Denial and Self-Love

I am to create a new order of humans, not sect mark you, but simply a new kind of humans - hurricane humans, who are devout believers in service and care nothing for worldly pleasures. Are you that human? If you are, then erase every bit of self from the soil of your mind and place society in its place. Empower yourself - empower yourself in thought, in feelings and above all in action. Give me hearts of honey, give me nerves of steel and I will revitalize the whole planet.

Hurricane humans are what I am here to create. Are you a hurricane human - no coward but a human who despite being in agonizing pain never for a second thinks about the self, but keeps on working for others, not as their leader, but as their servant? Are you such a being my friend? Remember, nobody will stand behind you if you put yourself as a leader, destroy the self first and the whole world will stand next to you.

Service begins where the self ends. But mark you, I am not talking about denial - to the real hurricane human destroying the self in the service of others is the greatest fulfillment of the self. Hence, denial is not even in the picture.

Self-denial and self-love are both creation of the self-obsessed mind. They are created by a materialist world in an attempt to justify selfishness.

Now I am not talking about hating yourself - all I am asking is to go beyond both self-denial and self-love and just let the self be, without all the judgmental norms and labels of the society. Self-love is a characteristic of the vain and self-denial of the meek. Both suffer from truthlessness - both suffer from the inability to accept reality as it is, hence they try to escape it either by denying the self or by making the self all-important.

If you are you, there is no question of denying the self or obsessing over the self, it's just the self being its natural self. Thesis and antithesis may try to depict such natural state of the self, but they only fail, for nature is beyond both thesis and anti-thesis.

Let me give you an example. You are reading right now what I am writing. I am putting the words on paper that are coming out of my mind. This simple act of wriiting is beyond both thesis and anti-thesis - I am neither denying myself nor loving myself - I am just letting the self be with no restraint of judgment whatsoever, hence the words keep flowing. Of course, once the final draft is finished, I will go through the entire manuscript and cancel out the factual, logical and emotional errors (by emotional errors I am referring to those statements that may be factually correct but they would be detrimental to the wellbeing of the society - not all facts are healthy for the society), if there are any, but that too is not an act of judgment, but an act of responsibility - responsibility which my words have towards the society.

You do your best work when you are you - you are not denying yourself or loving yourself - you are just being you - does the wind need to deny itself or love itself to blow across the lands - do the birds need to deny themselves or love themselves to chirp - likewise when the self is aware of itself, it needs not deny or love itself to be itself. And from that awareness rises responsibility - responsibility that automatically makes you conscientious enough to not do wrong to others - it's not self-denial, it's self-regulation.

Self-regulation is an intricate part of a healthy and progressive society. Self-regulation is conscience in action. And where there is conscience, there is civilization - no conscience, no civilization. But civilization doesn't mean fancy attires and pompous etiquettes, civilization means kind heart and unorthodox thinking. With the burial of each orthodox tradition, the road to progress and assimilation is smoothened further.

Progress alone won't do, it must have assimilation in it. In fact, progress without assimilation is no progress, but regress in disguise. What are you going to do with all the fancy apartments and sophisticated smart devices if you can't share your joys, sorrows, failures and achievements with people!

Remember, we can live without technology, but not without people. So, place people above everything else - above technology, above intellect, above religion, above nationality, above tradition, above culture, above ideology, and above politics. Nationality lost, nothing lost - religion lost, nothing lost - traditions lost, nothing lost - humanity lost, everything lost.

Now let's get back to the matter of self-denial. You must not confuse self-denial with self-annihilation, for self-annihilation is the state of mind where the self gets lost on its own due to its own natural tendency in the act of service. In annihilation the self finds salvation - that's service, nay that's human existence, for all other existence is animal existence. To live for others is human, to live for the self is animal. It's this simple. But again, this act of living as human can't be forced on a person, it can only be lived out of one's own genuine desire. It's better to live as an animal than a hypocrite.

However, I hold every human a traitor until they rush to the aid of those in distress. This is not charity - I say again and again - this is humanity. Humanity, that's the title we should be most attached to, yet that's the title we are least attached to. Why? Because no matter where you live, everybody is raised to be a loyal subject of one tribe or another. Harsh as it may sound, nobody is raised as a human, everybody is raised as a tribal animal. And as such they are given certain set of ideals to abide by their whole life without question. They are taught, may not be in words but in action, that tribalism is good and to be human is bad.

Very few parents, if any, actually take it upon themselves to go against the contemporary norms of the society to instill humanity in their kids above the tribal labels of societal barbarism. Society calls its labels culture, I call them savagery. And to such society I say, in a modern and global world, if you still can't bury your tribal inklings, you have no right to call yourself human. Call yourself human only when you actually start acting human, not before.

15. Either Diplomacy or Peace

I do not believe in a society that teaches tribalism - I do not believe in a society that teaches selfishness - I do not believe in a society that teaches shallowness. Society ought to be humane - society ought to be compassionate - society ought to be accountable - only then its acts will breed harmony and contentment, otherwise no matter how many united nations are formed, they cannot stop a single war from spilling innocent blood.

To prevent bloodshed on earth is the responsibility of every single human. It's your responsibility, it's my responsibility, it's our responsibility, not just of some fancy organizations full of figureheads. Diplomacy won't bring peace, only heartfelt nonjudgmental conversation will. So, for once O Nations of Earth, forget your national insecurities and sit down together, not as nations but as humans, not to negotiate, but to communicate. To be heard you must first listen.

Every nation has its strongholds as well as shortcomings. All you gotta do is embrace each other's strongholds and cancel out each other's shortcomings. But this is easier said than done, mostly because the so-called smart governments of earth would rather go to war with each other than acknowledge their flaws. And you can't create a peaceful global society without admitting your flaws and weaknesses.

Denying weakness may have been an effective quality for our tribal ancestors but it can't be a quality of a healthy human society. So my dear nations of earth, acknowledge your flaws, admit your weaknesses, announce it to the whole world, and your innocence alone will build the trust that all your diplomatic strategies couldn't. An hour of innocence builds more trust than years of diplomacy.

Any act that has deceit at its foundation can never instill peace in society. And diplomacy is founded upon the very element of deceit. Then how can a rational human possibly think that diplomacy will bring peace on earth! It never can - it never will. Deceit only breeds war, not peace. Hence, diplomacy may temporarily postpone war, but in the long run, it only breeds war, not peace.

So, when faced by an international conflict, forget diplomacy, forget statecraft, forget strategies and policies and ask yourself, what would a human do in this situation, not a politician, not a bureaucrat, not a law enforcement official, but a human? The tree of diplomacy only grows thorns of war, not fruits of peace.

If you want to instill peace on earth, then you must let go of your diplomatic tenets and start thinking as a plain, ordinary, conscientious human. Otherwise, centuries will pass, and still humankind will stay baffled by the concept of peace. Mark this, there is no time for diplomacy any more. Peace is urgent - peace is imperative, as imperative as the air we breathe and the water we drink. If you still can't feel this in your bones, then I am painstricken to say, catastrophe is awaiting your children.

Diplomats sitting inside their cozy air-conditioned offices most profoundly utter, you must have patience to have peace on earth. To them I say, how dare you preach on peace, you ignorant snobs - tell that to the innocent little kids who are suffering in warzones, without any clue as to whether they'll live to see the next day - while the capitalist circle of the developed world keeps getting richer by getting the shallow masses hooked on nonessential technology, these children of war have one question in their mind - whether starvation will kill them first or explosives. Shame on you - shame on us - who despite having a roof over head and food on the table, have not the slightest bit of concern for these innocent lives forgotten by destiny.

There is no time for patience - there is no time for diplomacy - there is no time for policies, legislations and meaningless paperwork. It's enough already. Either stand up and rush to the aid of these war-stricken communities through whichever means possible or keep your mouth shut for the rest of your life.

Soon the day will come when only the children of billionaires will have the right to a healthy and prosperous life, and all the other children will simply be lost in the cruel exploits of politics and consumerism. If you do not change, then no amount of humanitarian organizations will be able to fix the broken society of ours.

Change - I beg you - change for your children - for their health, sanity and prosperity. Stop buying every single new nonessential technology - stop wasting electricity - stop wasting fuel on carefree long drives - stop voting candidates impressed by their charm. Be responsible, be conscientious, act human, that is, if you do not want to hand over a messed up world to your children.

16. Time to Be Human

Breeding children is easy, but building a world suitable for their growth and prosperity is the real challenge. And I won't ask you - are you up for that challenge! Because if you are not, it means you do not give a damn about what happens to your children. And a mere human cannot reason with such savage callousness. So, what will it be - will you stand up as a human and take charge to right the wrongs of this world, or will you continue crawling as pesky, purposeless pest? The choice is yours, but the repercussions will follow your children and all the children to come for the rest of their lives.

You will be gone and your children will be left to deal with your mess - don't make a mess - make amends instead, for that's the right thing to do - that's the human thing to do. Our ancestors didn't know better, but we do, don't we! So, think better than our ancestors did - do better than our ancestors did - live better than our ancestors did. But mark you, living better doesn't mean living with comfort - living better means living with a concern for others.

If life is to be defined, let it be defined by acts of assimilation - if thought is to be defined, let it be defined by acts of conscience - if feelings are to be defined, let them be defined by acts of compassion. Let every element of life be defined by action - by practice, and not theory. And let that action be humane - let it be just - let it be inclusive - and not bigoted, discriminatory and inhuman. Let life be redefined through your footsteps. Carve out a new meaning of life - radiant and undying. One individual in one neighborhood, that's enough to change the world. The question is, why can't you be that individual?

I gave my youth to humanity, the most precious gift anybody could offer - but I am not asking you to do the same - all I am asking is step up wherever you see injustice - step up wherever you see bigotry - step up wherever you see savagery. Speak up against prejudice - speak up against hate crime - speak up against phobia (the social ones, not the clinical ones) - speak up against fundamentalism - speak up against excessive consumerism (for consumption is necessary, but consume what you need, not more than that) - speak up against climate change denial - speak up against anti-human act of any kind. It's time to teach humanity to the humans - and you are the one who can do that -

don't look for action in others - look at yourself - feel the unfelt, think the unthought, do the undone.

Norms and traditions mean nothing - that is they have no relation to truth, justice and righteousness - they are just there to serve as archetypes of social paradigms - they are there to ensure comfort of the people in the current societal structure. The purpose of norms and traditions are neither understanding, nor harmony, or progress. Traditions bring comfort not progress.

However, I am not saying that we should get rid of all traditions, rather what I am pointing out is that, we must never deem traditions to be all-important and people to be secondary. We must place people first, then traditions, and that too only those traditions that do not harm the society in any manner - and the rest we must throw as far away as possible.

Let no tradition teach you that you are superior and other people are inferior - let no traditions teach you that you are the greatest and other people are insignificant. Any book, any ritual, any ceremony, any text that preaches such narcissistic barbarism must be discarded at once. You must destroy every single trace of separatism from your society. Do not accept them, no matter what, even if you have to go against your own culture.

Even if your nation or your culture or your community is great at many things, you must never - I repeat, you must never boast about them as signs of your greatness. Remember, the greats never boast their greatness, only the roaches do that. And unfortunately, the world is filled with such roaches. Nevertheless, this mustn't dishearten you, because it's more reason for you to be the embodiment of humility that the world lacks.

The story of each human is the story of every human. So, turn your life into a story of kindness and amalgamation. Remember, you are the people's destiny. And each footstep of yours will turn into a flood of goodness that'll wash away all darkness from the face of earth - that'll wash away all wars - that'll wash away all injustice - that'll wash away all sectarianism - that'll wash away all inhumanities, primitive and modern alike.

BIBLIOGRAPHY

Aristotle. Politics. Penguin; Revised, Reprint edition. (2000)

Aristotle. De Anima (On the Soul). Penguin Random House. 1987

Aristotle. Physics. Kessinger Publishing, 2004

Archer M., (2000), Being Human: The Problem of Agency. Cambridge University Press.

Archer M., (2003), Structure, Agency and the Internal Conversation. Cambridge University Press.

Adolphs R (2003) Cognitive neuroscience of human social behaviour. Nature Rev Neurosci 4: 165–178.

Adolphs R, Tranel D, Damasio AR (2003) Dissociable neural systems for recognizing emotions. Brain Cogn 52: 61–69.

Afton, A. D. (1985). Forced copulation as a reproductive strategy of male lesser scaup: A field test of some predictions. - Behaviour 92, p. 146-167.

Allison T, Puce A, McCarthy G. (2000) Social perception from visual cues: role of the STS region. Trends Cogn Sci 4: 267–278.

Andresen, Jensine, and Robert Forman, eds. Cognitive Models and Spiritual Maps. Bowling Green, Ohio: Imprint Academic, 2000.

Ashbrook, James, and Carol Albright. The Humanizing Brain: Where Religion and Neuroscience Meet. Cleveland, OH: Pilgrim Press, 1997.

Azari, Nina, Janpeter Nickel, Gilbert Wunderlich, Michael Niedeggen, Harald Hefter, Lutz Tellmann, Hans Herzog, Petra Stoerig, Dieter Birnbacher, and Rudiger Seitz. "Neural Correlates of Religious Experience."

European Journal of Neuroscience 13, no. 8 (2001)

Agar, N. (2004). Liberal eugenics: In defence of human enhancement. London: Blackwell Publishing.

Alteheld, N., Roessler, G., Vobig, M., & Walter, R. (2004). The retina implant new approach to a visual prosthesis. Biomedizinische Technik, 49(4), 99–103.

Antal, A., Nitsche, M. A., Kincses, T. Z., Kruse, W., Hoffmann, K. P., & Paulus, W. (2004a). Facilitation of visuo-motor learning by transcranial direct current stimulation of the motor and extrastriate visual areas in humans. European Journal of Neuroscience, 19(10), 2888–2892.

Bhat Z, Kumar, S, Bhat H (2015) In vitro meat production. Challenges and benefits over conventional meat production. J Sci Food Agric 14: 241–248

Bernstein R. J., (1967), John Dewey. New York: Washington Square Press.

Bernstein R.J., (1971), Praxis and Action: Contemporary Philosophies of Human Activity. Philadelphia: University of Pennsylvania Press.

Bernstein R.J., (1976), The Restructuring Social and Political Thought.

Bernstein R.J., (1983), Beyond Relativism and Objectivism: Science, Hermeneutics, and Praxis. Philadelphia: University of Pennsylvania Press.

Bernstein R.J., (1986), Philosophical Profiles. Philadelphia: University of Pennsylvania Press.

Bernstein R.J., (1991), New Constellation. Cambridge: MIT Press.

Barash, D. P. (1977). Sociobiology of rape in mallards (Anas platyrhynchos):

Responses of the mated male. - Science 197, p. 788-789.

Berger, J. (1986). Wild horses of the great basin: Social competition and population size. - The University of Chicago Press, Chicago.

Birkhead, T. R., Johnson, S. D. & Nettleship, D. N. (1985). Extra-pair matings and mate guarding in the common murre Uria aalge. - Anim. Behav. 33, p. 608-619.

Beauregard, Mario, and Vincent Paquette. "Neural Correlates of a Mystical Experience in Carmelite Nuns." Neuroscience Letters 405, no. 3 (2006)

Benson, Herbert. Timeless Healing: The Power and Biology of Belief. New York: Scribner, 1996

Bogen, J.E.(1995a), 'On the neurophysiology of consciousness: Part I. An overview', Consciousness and Cognition, 4.

Bogen, J.E. (1995b), 'On the neurophysiology of consciousness: Part II. Constraining the semantic problem', Consciousness and Cognition, 4.

Bremner, J. D., R. Soufer, et al. (2001). "Gender differences in cognitive and neural correlates of remembrance of emotional words." Psychopharmacol Bull 35 (3).

Brothers, L. (2002). The social brain: A project for integrating primate behavior and neurophysiology in a new domain. In J. T. Cacioppo et al. (Eds.), Foundations in neuroscience. Cambridge, MA: MIT Press.

Buss, D. D. (2003). Evolutionary Psychology: The New Science of Mind, 2nd ed. New York: Allyn & Bacon.

Buss, D. M. (1989). "Conflict between the sexes: Strategic interference and the evocation of anger and upset." J Pers Soc Psychol 56 (5).

Buss, D. M. (1995). "Psychological sex differences. Origins through sexual selection." Am Psychol 50 (3).

Buss, D. M. (2002). "Review: Human Mate Guarding." Neuro Endocrinol Lett 23 (Suppl 4).

Buss, D. M., and D. P. Schmitt (1993). "Sexual strategies theory: An evolutionary perspective on human mating." Psychol Rev 100 (2).

Blakemore SJ, Decety J (2001) From the perception of action to the understanding of intention. Nature Rev Neurosci 2: 561.

Bruce C, Desimone R, Gross CG (1981) Visual properties of neurons in a polysensory area in superior temporal sulcus of the macaque. J Neurophysiol 46: 369–384.

Buccino G, Vogt S, Ritzl A, Fink GR, Zilles K, Freund HJ, Rizzolatti G (2004) Neural circuits underlying imitation of hand actions: an event related fMRI study. Neuron 42: 323–34.

Colapietro V., (1988), "Human Agency: The Habits of Our Being." Southern Journal of Philosophy, XXVI, 2, pp. 153-68.

Colapietro V., (1992), "Purpose, Power, and Agency." The Monist, 75, 4 (October) pp. 423-44.

Colapietro V., (2003), "Signs and their vicissitudes: Meanings in excess of consciousness and functionality." Logica, Dialogica, Ideologica, a cure di Susan Petrilli e Patrizia Calefato (Milano: Mimesis), pp. 221-36.

Colapietro V., (2004a), "C. S. Peirce's Reclamation of Teleology." Nature in American Philosophy, ed. Jean De Groot (Washington, D.C.: Catholic University Press of America), pp. 88-108.

Colapietro V., (2004b), "Portrait of a Historicist: An Alternative Reading of

Peircean Semiotic." Semiotiche, 2/04 [maggio 2004], pp. 49-68.

Colapietro V., (2006), "Engaged Pluralism: Between Alterity and Sociality." The Pragmatic Century: Conversations with Richard J. Bernstein (Albany, NY: SUNY Press), pp. 39-68.

Colapietro V., (2009), "Habit, Competence, and Purpose." Forthcoming in The Transactions of the Charles S. Peirce Society. Calder AJ, Keane J, Manes F, Antoun N, Young AW (2000) Impaired recognition and experience of disgust following brain injury. Nature Neurosci 3: 1077–1078.

Carey DP, Perrett DI, Oram MW (1997) Recognizing, understanding and reproducing actions. In: Jeannerod M, Grafman J (eds) Handbook of neuropsychology. Vol. 11: Action and cognition. Elsevier, Amsterdam.

Carr L, Iacoboni M, Dubeau MC, Mazziotta JC, Lenzi GL (2003) Neural mechanisms of empathy in humans: a relay from neural systems for imitation to limbic areas. Proc Natl Acad Sci USA 100: 5497–5502.

Changeux JP, Ricoeur P (1998) La nature et la règle. Odile Jacob, Paris.

Cochin S, Barthelemy C, Roux S, Martineau J (1999) Observation and execution of movement: similarities demonstrated by quantified electroencephalograpy. Eur J Neurosci 11: 1839– 1842.

Chomsky Noam, (2017) Requiem for the American Dream

Chomsky Noam, (2016) Who Rules the World?

Chomsky Noam, (2010) How the World Works

Churchland, P.S. (1986), Neurophilosophy (Cambridge, MA: The MIT Press).

Churchland, P.S. & Ramachandran, V.S. (1993), 'Filling in: Why Dennett is wrong', in Dennett and His Critics: Demystifying Mind, ed. B. Dahlbom (Oxford: Blackwell Scientific Press).

Churchland, P.S., Ramachandran, V.S. & Sejnowski, T.J. (1994), 'A critique of pure vision', in Large- scale Neuronal Theories of the Brain, ed. C. Koch & J.L. Davis (Cambridge, MA: The MIT Press).

Crick, F. (1994), The Astonishing Hypothesis: The Scientific Search for the Soul (New York: Simon and Schuster).

Crick, F. (1996), 'Visual perception: rivalry and consciousness', Nature, 379.

Crick, F. & Koch, C. (1992), 'The problem of consciousness', Scientific American, 267.

Craig AD (2002) How do you feel? Interoception: the sense of the physiological condition of the body. Nature Rev Neurosci 3: 655–666.

Damasio, A (2003a) Looking for Spinoza. Harcourt Inc. Damasio A (2003b) Feeling of emotion and the self. Ann NY Acad Sci 1001: 253–261.

d'Aquili, Eugene. "Senses of Reality in Science and Religion." Zygon 17, no 4 (1982)

d'Aquili, Eugene. "The Biopsychological Determinants of Religious Ritual Behavior." Zygon 10, no. 1 (1975)

d'Aquili, Eugene. "The Myth-Ritual Complex: A Biogenetic Structural Analysis." Zygon 18, no. 3 (1983) d'Aquili, Eugene, and Andrew Newberg. The Mystical Mind: Probing the Biology of Religious Experience. Minneapolis: Fortress Press, 1999.

Daly DD. 1958. Ictal affect. Am J Psychiatry.

Damasio, A. (1994) Descartes' Error: Emotion, Reason and the Human Brain. New York, Putnams.

Damasio, A. (1999) The Feeling of What Happens: Body, Emotion and the Making of Consciousness. London, Heinemann.

Darwin, C. (1859) On the Origin of Species by Means of Natural Selection. London, Murray.

Darwin, C. (1871) The Descent of Man and Selection in Relation to Sex. London, John Murray.

Darwin, C. (1872) The Expression of the Emotions in Man and Animals. London, John Murray; also published

1965, Chicago, University of Chicago Press.

Dawkins, M.S. (1987) Minding and mattering. In C. Blakemore and S. Greenfield (eds) Mindwaves. Oxford, Blackwell, 151-60.

Dawkins, R. (1976) The Selfish Gene. Oxford, Oxford University Press; a new edition, with additional material, was published in 1989.

Dawkins, R. (1986) The Blind Watchmaker. London, Longman.

Di Pellegrino G, Fadiga L, Fogassi L, Gallese V, Rizzolatti G (1992) Understanding motor events: A neurophysiological study. Exp Brain Res 91: 176–80.

Deikman, A.J. (2000) A functional approach to mysticism. Journal of Consciousness Studies 7(11-12), 75-91.

Delmonte, M.M. (1987) Personality and meditation. In M. West (ed.) The

Psychology of Meditation. Oxford, Clarendon Press, 118-32.

Dennett, D.C. (1987) The Intentional Stance. Cambridge, MA, MIT Press.

Dennett, D.C. (1988) Quining qualia. In A.J. Marcel and E. Bisiach (eds) Consciousness in Contemporary Science. Oxford, Oxford University Press, 42-77.

Dennett, D.C. (1991) Consciousness Explained. Boston, MA, and London, Little, Brown and Co.

Dennett, D.C. (1995a) Darwin's Dangerous Idea. London, Penguin.

Dennett, D.C. (1995b) The unimagined preposterousness of zombies. Journal of Consciousness Studies 2(4), 322-6.

Dennett, D.C. (1995c) Cog: steps towards consciousness in robots. In T. Metzinger (ed.) Conscious Experience. Thorverton, Devon, Imprint Academic, 471-87.

Dennett, D.C. (1995d) The path not taken. Behavioral and Brain Sciences 18, 252-3; commentary on N. Block, On a confusion about a function of consciousness. Behavioral and Brain Sciences 18, 227.

Dennett, D.C. (1996a) Facing backwards on the problem of consciousness. Journal of Consciousness Studies 3(1), 4-6.

Dennett, D.C. (1996b) Kinds of Minds: Towards an Understanding of Consciousness. London, Weidenfeld & Nicolson.

Dennett, D.C. (1997) An exchange with Daniel Dennett. In J. Searle (ed.) The Mystery of Consciousness. New York, New York Review of Books, 115-19.

Dennett, D.C. (1998) The myth of double transduction. In S.R. Hameroff, A.W. Kaszniak and A. C. Scott (eds) Toward a Science of Consciousness: The Second Tucson Discussions and

Debates. Cambridge, MA, MIT Press, 97-107.

Dennett, D.C. (1998b) Brainchildren: Essays on Designing Minds. Cambridge, MA, MIT Press.

Dennett, D.C. (2001) The fantasy of first person science. Debate with D. Chalmers, Northwestern University, Evanston, IL, February 2001.

Dennett, D.C. (2003) Freedom Evolves. New York, Penguin.

Dennett, D.C. and Kinsbourne, M. (1992) Time and the observer: the where and when of consciousness in the brain. Behavioral and Brain Sciences 15, 183-247, including commentaries and authors' responses.

Dewey J., (1911 [1977]), "Epistemological Realism: The Alleged Ubiquity of the Knowledge Relation." Journal of Philosophy, VIII, 20 (September 28, 1911).

Dewhurst, Kenneth, and A. W. Beard. "Sudden Religious Conversions in Temporal Lobe Epilepsy." British Journal of Psychiatry 117 (1970)

Dewhurst K, Beard AW. Sudden religious conversions in temporal lobe epilepsy. 1970 Epilepsy Behav 2003

Devinsky O, Lai G. Spirituality and religion in epilepsy. Epilepsy Behav 2008.

Devinsky, O., Morrell, MJ, Vogt, BA. (1995) 'Contribution of anterior cingulate cortex to behavior', Brain, 118.

Douglas Stone A., Chapter 24, The Indian Comet, in the book Einstein and the Quantum, Princeton University Press, Princeton, New Jersey, 2013.

E. Horvitz, "One Hundred Year Study on Artificial Intelligence: Reflections and Framing," ed: Stanford University, 2014.

Einstein A. (1925). "Quantentheorie des einatomigen idealen Gases". Sitzungsberichte der Preussischen Akademie der Wissenschaften.

Eckhart Meister, Selected Writings

Egidi R., ed. (1999), "Von Wright and 'Dante's Dream': Stages in a Philosophical Pilgrim's Progress", in In Search of a New Humanism: the Philosophy of G.H. von Wright, ed. by R. Egidi, Kluwer, Dordrecht.

Fadiga L, Fogassi L, Pavesi G, Rizzolatti G (1995) Motor facilitation during action observation: a magnetic stimulation study. J Neurophysiol 73: 2608–2611.

Fogassi L, Gallese V, Fadiga L, Rizzolatti G (1998) Neurons responding to the sight of goal directed hand/arm actions in the parietal area PF (7b) of the macaque monkey. Soc Neurosci Abs 24:257.5.

Frith U, Frith CD (2003) Development and neurophysiology of mentalizing. Philos Trans R Soc Lond B Biol Sci 358: 459.

Farah, M.J. (1989), 'The neural basis of mental imagery', Trends in Neurosciences, 10.

Finlay BL, Darlington RB (1995) Linked regularities in the development and evolution of mammalian brains. Science 268.

Freud, S. "The Interpretation of Dreams", 1900

Freud, S. "Selected papers on hysteria and other psychoneuroses" Journal of Nervous and Mental Disease 1909.

Freud, S. "The Origin and Development of Psychoanalysis", 1910

Freud, S. "Psychopathology of everyday life", 1914

Freud, S. "Beyond the Pleasure Principle", 1920

Frith, C.D. & Dolan, R.J. (1997), 'Abnormal beliefs: Delusions and memory', Paper presented at the May, 1997, Harvard Conference on Memory and Belief.

Gay, Volney, ed. Neuroscience and Religion. Plymouth, UK: Lexington Books, 2009.

Gazzaniga, M. S. (1985). The social brain. New York: Basic Books.

Gazzaniga, M.S. (1993), 'Brain mechanisms and conscious experience', Ciba Foundation Symposium, 174.

Geschwind N. "Behavioural changes in temporal lobe epilepsy". Psychol Med. 1979.

Gellhorn, E., Kiely, W.F. "Mystical states of consciousness: neurophysiological and clinical aspects." J Nerv Ment Dis. 1972;154:399-405.

Gilbert SL, Dobyns WB, Lahn BT (2005) Genetic links between brain development and brain evolution. Nat Rev Genet 6.

Gray JA. The Psychology of Fear and Stress. 2nd ed. New York, NY: Cambridge University Press; 1988.

Gloor, P. (1992), 'Amygdala and temporal lobe epilepsy', in The Amygdala: Neurobiological Aspects of Emotion, Memory and Mental Dysfunction, ed J.P. Aggleton (New York: Wiley-Liss).

Greenspan, S. I. and S. G. Shanker (2004). The first idea: How symbols, language, and intelligence evolved from our early primate ancestors to modern humans. Cambridge, MA: Da Capo Press.

Grady, D. (1993), 'The vision thing: Mainly in the brain', Discover, June.

Gallagher HL, Frith CD (2003) Functional imaging of 'theory of mind'. Trends Cogn Sci 7: 77.

Gallese V, Fogassi L, Fadiga L, Rizzolatti G (2002) Action representation and the inferior parietal lobule. In: Prinz W, Hommel B (eds) Attention & Performance XIX. Common mechanisms in perception and action. Oxford University Press, Oxford.

Gallese V, Keysers C, Rizzolatti G (2004) A unifying view of the basis of social cognition. Trends Cogn Sci 8: 396–403.

Gangitano M, Mottaghy FM, Pascual-Leone A (2001) Phase specific modulation of cortical motor output during movement observation. NeuroReport 12: 1489–1492.

Gangitano M, Mottaghy FM, Pascual-Leone A (2004) Modulation of premotor mirror neuron activity during observation of unpredictable grasping movements. Eur J Neurosci 20: 2193– 2202.

Goldman AI, Sripada CS (2004) Simulationist models of face-based emotion recognition. Cognition 94: 193–213.

Grèzes J, Costes N, Decety J (1998) Top-down effect of strategy on the perception of human biological motion: a PET investigation. Cogn Neuropsychol 15: 553–582.

Grèzes J, Armony JL, Rowe J, Passingham RE (2003) Activations related to "mirror" and "canonical" neurones in the human brain: an fMRI study. Neuroimage 18: 928–937.

Gross CG, Rocha-Miranda CE, Bender DB (1972) Visual properties of neurons in the inferotemporal cortex of the macaque. J Neurophysiol 35: 96–111.

Hari R, Forss N, Avikainen S, Kirveskari S, Salenius S, Rizzolatti G

(1998) Activation of human primary motor cortex during action observation: a neuromagnetic study. Proc. Natl Acad Sci USA 95: 15061–15065.

Hardy, G. H. (1940). Ramanujan. Cambridge: Cambridge University Press.

Hall, Daniel, Keith Meador, and Harold Koenig. "Measuring Religiousness in Health Research: Review and Critique." Journal of Religion and Health 47, no. 2 (2008)

Harris, Sam, Jonas Kaplan, Ashley Curiel, Susan Bookheimer, Marco Iacoboni, and Mark Cohen. "The Neural Correlates of Religious and Nonreligious Belief." PLoS One 4, no. 10 (October 1, 2009)

Halgren, E. (1992), 'Emotional neurophysiology of the amygdala within the context of human cognition', in The Amygdala:

Neurobiological Aspects of Emotion, Memory and Mental Dysfunction, ed J.P. Aggleton (New York: Wiley-Liss).

Halligan PW, Fink GR, Marshal JC, Vallar G. 2003. Spatial cognition: evidence from visual neglect. Trends Cogn Sci.

Handbook of Emotions, Edited by Michael Lewis, Jeannette M. Haviland-Jones, and Lisa Feldman Barrett, The Guilford Press; 3rd edition (2010).

Haggard, P., Clark, S. and Kalogeras,]. (2002) Voluntary action and conscious awareness, Nature Neuroscience 5, 382-5. Haggard, P., Newman, C. and Magno, E. (1999) On the perceived time of voluntary actions. British Journal of Psychology 90, 291-303.

Hameroff, S.R. and Penrose, R. (1996) Conscious events as orchestrated space-time selections. Journal of Consciousness Studies 3(1), 36-53; also reprinted in J. Shear (ed.) (1997)

Explaining Consciousness-The Hard Problem. Cambridge, MA, MIT Press, 177-95.

Hardcastle, V.G. (2000) How to understand theN in NCC. InT. Metzinger (ed.) Neural Correlates of Consciousness. Cambridge, MA, MIT Press, 259-64.

Harding, D.E. (1961) On Having no Head: Zen and the Re-Discovery of the Obvious. London, Buddhist Society.

Hardy, A. (1979) The Spiritual Nature of Man: A Study of Contemporary Religious Experience. Oxford, Clarendon Press.

Hamad, S. (1990) The symbol grounding problem. Physica D 42, 335-46.

Hamad, S. (2001) No easy way out. The Sciences 41(2), 36-42.

Harre, R. and Gillett, G. (1994) The Discursive Mind. Thousand Oaks, CA, Sage.

Haugeland, J. (ed.) (1997) Mind Design II: Philosophy, Psychology, Artificial Intelligence. Cambridge, MA, MIT Press.

Hauser, M.D. (2000) Wild Minds: What Animals Really Think. New York, Henry Holt and Co.; London, Penguin.

Hearne, K. (1990) The Dream Machine. Northants, Aquarian.

Hebb, D.O. (1949) The Organization of Behavior. New York, Wiley.

Helmholtz, H.L.F. von (1856-67) Treatise on Physiological Optics.

Hess, EH (1975) "The role of pupil size in communication," Scientific American, 233(5), 110–12.

Heyes, C.M. (1998) Theory of mind in nonhuman primates. Behavioral and

Brain Sciences 21, 101-48; with commentaries.

Heyes, C.M. and Galef, B.G. (eds) (1996) Social Learning in Animals: The Roots of Culture. San Diego, CA, Academic Press.

Hilgard, E.R. (1986) Divided Consciousness: Multiple Controls in Human Thought and Action. New York, Wiley.

Hocquette JF (2016) Is in vitro meat the

solution for the future? Meat Science 120:

167–176

Hodgson, R. (1891) A case of double consciousness. Proceedings of the Society for Psychical Research 7, 221-58.

Hofstadter, D.R. (1979) Code!, Escher, Bach: An Eternal Golden Braid. London, Penguin.

Hofstadter, D.R. and Dennett, D.C. (eds) (1981) The Mind's I: Fantasies and Reflections on Self and Soul. London, Penguin.

Holland, J. (ed.) (2001) Ecstasy: The Complete Guide: A Comprehensive Look at the Risks and Benefits of MDMA. Rochester, VT, Park Street Press.

Holmes, D.S. (1987) The influence of meditation versus rest on physiological arousal. In M. West (ed.) The Psychology of Meditation. Oxford, Clarendon Press, 81-103.

Holt, J. (1999) Blindsight in debates about qualia. Journal of Consciousness Studies 6(5), 54-71.

Horgan, J. (1994), 'Can science explain consciousness?', Scientific American, 271.

Holloway RL (1996) Evolution of the human brain. In: Lock A, Peters CR (eds) Handbook of human symbolic evolution. Oxford University Press, Oxford

Iacoboni M, Woods RP, Brass M, Bekkering H, Mazziotta JC, Rizzolatti G (1999) Cortical mechanisms of human imitation. Science 286: 2526–2528.

Iacoboni M, Koski LM, Brass M, Bekkering H, Woods RP, Dubeau MC, Mazziotta JC, Rizzolatti G (2001) Reafferent copies of imitated actions in the right superior temporal cortex. Proc Natl Acad Sci USA 98: 13995–13999.

Jeannerod M (1988) The neural and behavioural organization of goal-directed movements. Clarendon Press, Oxford.

Johnson-Frey SH, Maloof FR, Newman-Norlund R, Farrer C, Inati S, Grafton ST (2003) Actions or hand-objects interactions? Human inferior frontal cortex and action observation. Neuron 39: 1053–1058.

Jackson, F. (1982) Epiphenomenal qualia. Philosophical Quarterly 32, 127-36.

James, W. (1890) The Principles of Psychology (2 volumes). London, Macmillan.

James, W. (1902) The Varieties of Religious Experience: A Study in Human Nature. New York and London, Longmans, Green and Co.

Jansen, K. (2001) Ketamine: Dreams and Realities. Sarasota, FL, Multidisciplinary Association for Psychedelic Studies.

Jay, M. (ed.) (1999) Artificial Paradises: A Drugs Reader. London, Penguin.

Jaynes, J. (1976) The Origin of Consciousness in the Breakdown of the Bicameral Mind. New York, Houghton Mifflin.

Johnson, M.K. and Raye, C.L. (1981) Reality monitoring. Psychological Review 88, 67-85.

Kadim I, Mahgoub O, Baqir S et al. (2015) Cultured meat from muscle stem cells: a review of challenges and prospects. J Integr Agr 14: 222–233

Koski L, Iacoboni M, Dubeau MC, Woods RP, Mazziotta JC (2003) Modulation of cortical activity during different imitative behaviors. J Neurophysiol 89: 460–471.

Krolak-Salmon P, Henaff MA, Isnard J, Tallon-Baudry C, Guenot M, Vighetto A, Bertrand O, Mauguiere F (2003) An attention modulated response to disgust in human ventral anterior insula. Ann Neurol 53: 446–453.

Kandel, E. R. In Search of Memory: The Emergence of a New Science of Mind, W. W. Norton & Company (2007).

Kandel E. R. Schwartz JH, Jessel TM. Principles of neural sciences. New York; McGraw Hill, 2000.

Kanizsa, G. (1979), Organization In Vision (New York: Praeger).

Kaloupek DG, Scott JR, Khatami V. Assessment of coping strategies associated with syncope in blood donors. J Psychosom Res. 1985;29:207-214.

Kanwisher, N. (2001) Neural events and perceptual awareness. Cognition 79, 89-113; also reprinted inS. Dehaene (ed.) The Cognitive Neuroscience of Consciousness. Cambridge, MA, MIT Press, 89-113.

Kapleau, Roshi P. (1980) The Three Pillars of Zen: Teaching, Practice, and Enlightenment (revised edn). New York, Doubleday.

Karn, K. and Hayhoe, M. (2000) Memory representations guide

targeting eye movements in a natural task. Visual Cognition 7, 673-703.

Kasamatsu, A. and Hirai, T. (1966) An electroencephalographic study on the Zen meditation (zazen). Folia Psychiatrica et Neurologica Japonica 20, 315-36.

Kaiserman-Abramof, I. R., Graybiel, A. M., & Nauta, W. J. (1980). The thalamic projection to cortical area 17 in a congenitally anophthalmic mouse strain. Neuroscience, 5, 41–52.

Kanold, P. O., Kara, P., Reid, R. C., & Shatz, C. J. (2003). Role of subplate neurons in functional maturation of visual cortical columns. Science, 301, 521–525.

Kennedy, H., & Dehay, C. (1988). Functional implications of the anatomical organization of the callosal projections of visual areas V1 and V2 in the macaque monkey. Behav. Brain Res., 29, 225–236.

Kentridge, R.W. and Heywood, C.A. (1999) The status of blindsight. Journal of Consciousness Studies 6(5), 3-11.

Kihlstrom, J.F. (1996) Perception without awareness of what is perceived, learning without awareness of what is learned. In M. Velmans (ed.) The Science of Consciousness. London, Routledge, 23-46.

Kollerstrom, N. (1999) The path of Halley's comet, and Newton's late apprehension of the law of gravity. Annals of Science 56, 331-56.

Kosslyn, S.M. (1980) Image and Mind. Cambridge, MA, Harvard University Press.

Kosslyn, S.M. (1988) Aspects of a cognitive neuroscience of mental imagery. Science 240, 1621-6.

Kinsbourne, M. (1995), 'The intralaminar thalamic nucleii', Consciousness and Cognition, 4.

Kjaer, Troels, Camilla Bertelsen, Paola Piccini, David Brooks, Jorgen Alving, and Hans Lou. "Increased Dopamine Tone during Meditation- Induced Change of Consciousness." Cognitive Brain Research 13, no. 2 (April 2002)

Kölmel HW. 1985. Complex visual hallucinations in the hemianopic field. J Neurol Neurosurg Psychiatry.

Koenig, Harold. "Research on Religion, Spirituality, and Mental Health: A Review." Canadian Journal of Psychiatry 54, no. 5 (May 2009)

Koenig, Harold, ed. Handbook of Religion and Mental Health. San Diego, CA: Academic Press, 1998

Kraepelin E. Psychiatry: A Textbook for Students and Physicians. New York, NY: Science History Publications; 1990.

Lauglin, Charles, John McManus, and Eugene d'Aquili. Brain, Symbol, and

Experience. 2nd ed. New York: Columbia University Press, 1992

Lakoff, G. and M. Johnson (1999). Philosophy in the flesh. Basic Books: New York.

LeDoux, J. E. (1996). The emotional brain. New York: Simon & Schuster.

LeDoux, J.E. (1992), 'Emotion and the amygdala', in The Amygdala: Neurobiological Aspects of Emo- tion, Memory and Mental Dysfunction, ed J.P. Aggleton (New York: Wiley-Liss).

Levin, D.T. and Simons, D.J. (1997) Failure to detect changes to attended objects in motion pictures. Psychonomic Bulletin and Review 4, 501-6.

Levine,J. (1983) Materialism and qualia: the explanatory gap. Pacific Philosophical Quarterly 64, 354-61.

Levine,J. (2001) Purple Haze: The Puzzle of Consciousness. New York,

Oxford University Press. Levine, S. (1979) A Gradual Awakening. New York, Doubleday.

Levinson, B.W. (1965) States of awareness during general anaesthesia. British Journal of Anaesthesia 37, 544-6.

Lewicki, P., Czyzewska, M. and Hoffman, H. (1987) Unconscious acquisition of complex procedural knowledge. Journal of Experimental Psychology: Learning, Memory and Cognition 13, 523-30.

Lewicki, P., Hill, T. and Bizot, E. (1988) Acquisition of procedural knowledge about a pattern of stimuli that cannot be articulated. Cognitive Psychology 20, 24-37.

Lewicki, P., Hill, T. and Czyzewska, M. (1992) Nonconscious acquisition of information. American Psychologist 47, 796-801.

Manthey S, Schubotz RI, von Cramon DY (2003). Premotor cortex in observing erroneous action: an fMRI study. Brain Res Cogn Brain Res 15: 296–307.

Mesulam MM, Mufson EJ (1982) Insula of the old world monkey. III: Efferent cortical output and comments on function. J Comp Neurol 212: 38–52.

Naskar, Abhijit. "Homo: A Brief History of Consciousness", 2015

Naskar, Abhijit. "What is Mind?", 2016

Naskar, Abhijit. "In Search of Divinity: Journey to The Kingdom of Conscience", 2016

Naskar, Abhijit. "Love, God & Neurons: Memoir of A Scientist who found himself by getting lost", 2016

Naskar, Abhijit. "Neurons of Jesus: Mind of A Teacher, Spouse & Thinker", 2017

Naskar, Abhijit. "The Islamophobic Civilization: Voyage of Acceptance", 2017

Naskar, Abhijit. "Principia Humanitas", 2017

Naskar, Abhijit. "We Are All Black: A Treatise on Racism", 2017

Naskar, Abhijit. "Wise Mating: A Treatise on Monogamy", 2017

Naskar, Abhijit. "I Am The Thread: My Mission", 2017

Naskar, Abhijit. "The Bengal Tigress: A Treatise on Gender Equality", 2017

Naskar, Abhijit. "Build Bridges not Walls: In the name of Americana", 2018

Naskar, Abhijit. "Fabric of Humanity", 2018

Naskar, Abhijit. "Lives To Serve Before I Sleep", 2019

Naskar, Abhijit. "Citizens of Peace: Beyond the Savagery of Sovereignty", 2019

Naskar, Abhijit. "The Constitution of The United Peoples of Earth", 2019

Naskar, Abhijit. "Neurons Giveth, Neurons Taketh Away | Abhijit Naskar | TEDxIIMRanchi", 2019 https://www.youtube.com/watch?v=BNX-Q0ySm80

Naskar, Abhijit. "Mission Reality", 2019

Naskar, Abhijit. "Operation Justice: To Make A Society That Needs No Law", 2019

Naskar, Abhijit. "Every Generation Needs Caretakers: The Gospel of Patriotism", 2020

Naskar, Abhijit. "The Gospel of Technology", 2020

Naskar, Abhijit. "When Call The People: My World My Responsibility", 2020

Naskar, Abhijit. "No Foreigner Only Family", 2020

Newberg, Andrew, and Jeremy Iversen. "The Neural Basis of the Complex Mental Task of Meditation: Neurotransmitter and Neurochemical Considerations." Medical Hypotheses 61, no. 2 (2003).

Newberg, Andrew. "How God Changes Your Brain: An Introduction to Jewish Neurotheology", CCAR Journal: The Reform Jewish Quarterly, Winter 2016.

Newberg, Andrew, and Stephanie Newberg. "A Neuropsychological Perspective on Spiritual Development." In Handbook of Spiritual Development in Childhood and Adolescence, edited by Eugene Roehlkepartain, Pamela King, Linda

Wagener, and Peter Benson. London: Sage Publications, Inc., 2005

Newberg, Andrew. "The Neurotheology Link An Intersection Between Spirituality and Health", Alternative and Complimentary Therapies, Vol 21 No 1, February 2015.

Newberg, Andrew, Nancy Wintering, Dharma Khalsa, Hannah Roggenkamp, and Mark Waldman. "Meditation Effects on Cognitive Function and Cerebral Blood Flow in Subjects with Memory Loss: A Preliminary Study." Journal of Alzheimer's Disease 20, no. 2 (2010)

Nash, M. (1995), 'Glimpses of the mind', Time.

Nesse RM. Proximate and evolutionary studies of anxiety, stress and depression: synergy at the interface. Neurosci Biobehav Rev. 1999;23:895-903.

Nicolelis, Miguel. (2011) "Beyond Boundaries: The New Neuroscience of Connecting Brains with Machines---and How It Will Change Our Lives", Times Books

O'Hara, K. and Scutt, T. (1996) There is no hard problem of consciousness. Journal of Consciousness Studies 3(4), 290-302, reprinted in J. Shear (ed.) (1997) Explaining Consciousness. Cambridge, MA, MIT Press, 69-82.

O'Regan, J.K. (1992) Solving the "real" mysteries of visual perception: the world as an outside memory. Canadian Journal of Psychology 46, 461-88.

O'Regan, J.K. and Noe, A. (2001) A sensorimotor account of vision and visual consciousness. Behavioral and Brain Sciences 24(5), 883-917.

O'Regan, J.K., Rensink, R.A. and Clark,].]. (1999) Change-blindness as a result of "mudsplashes." Nature 398, 34.

Ornstein, R.E. (1977) The Psychology of Consciousness (2nd edn). New York, Harcourt.

Ornstein, R.E. (1986) The Psychology of Consciousness (3rd edn). New York, Pehguin.

Ornstein, R.E. (1992) The Evolution of Consciousness. New York, Touchstone.

Penfield W, Faulk ME (1955) The insula: further observations on its function. Brain 78: 445– 470.

Penrose, R. (1994), Shadows of the Mind (Oxford: Oxford University Press).

Penrose, R. (1989), The Emperor's New Mind: Concerning Computers, Minds and The Laws of Physics (Oxford: Oxford University Press).

Persinger, "'I would kill in God's name' role of sex, weekly church attendance, report of a religious experience and limbic lability" Perceptual and Motor Skills 1997.

Persinger "Experimental simulation of the God experience" Neurotheology 2003.

Persinger, M. A. (1993b). Personality changes following brain injury as a grief response to the loss of sense of self: Phenomenological themes as indices of local lability and neurocognitive restructuring as psycho- therapy. Psychological Reports, 72

Persinger, Corradini, Clement, Keaney, et al "Neurotheology and its convergence with neuroquantology" NeuroQuantology 2010.

Persinger, Koren and St-Pierre "The electromagnetic induction of mystical and altered states within the laboratory" Journal of Consciousness Exploration and Research 2010.

Persinger "Case report: A prototypical spontaneous 'sensed presence' of a sentient being and concomitant electroencephalographic activity in the clinical laboratory" Neurocase 2008.

Persinger and Saroka "Potential production of Hughlings Jackson's "parasitic consciousness" by physiologically-patterned weak transcerebral magnetic fields: QEEG and source localization" Epilepsy & Behavior 28 (2013).

Persinger. "The neuropsychiatry of paranormal experiences". J Neuropsychiatry Clin Neurosci 2001.

Persinger. "Neuropsychological bases of god beliefs", New York: Praeger, 1987

Persinger. "Temporal lobe epileptic signs and correlative behaviors displayed by normal populations", Journal of General Psychology, 1986

Perry BD, Pollard R. Homeostasis, stress, trauma, and adaptation. A neurodevelopmental view of childhood trauma. Child Adolesc Psychiatr Clin N Am. 1998;7:33.

Paré, D. & Llinás, R. (1995), 'Conscious and preconscious processes as seen from the standpoint of sleep-waking cycle neurophysiology', Neuropsychologia, 33.

P. S. de Laplace. Essai Philosophique sur les Probabilites [1814], in Academy des Sciences, Oeuvres Complotes de Laplace, Vol. 7, Gauthier-Villars, Paris (1886).

Perrett DI, Harries MH, Bevan R, Thomas S, Benson PJ, Mistlin AJ, Chitty AJ, Hietanen JK, Ortega JE (1989) Frameworks of analysis for the neural representation of animate objects and actions. J Exp Bio 146: 87–113.

Phillips ML, Young AW, Senior C, Brammer M, Andrew C, Calder AJ, Bullmore ET, Perrett DI, Rowland D, Williams SC, Gray JA, David AS (1997) A specific neural substrate for perceiving facial expressions of disgust. Nature 389: 495–498.

Phillips ML, Young AW, Scott SK, Calder AJ, Andrew C, Giampietro V, Williams SC, Bullmore ET, Brammer M, Gray JA (1998) Neural responses to facial and vocal expressions of fear and disgust. Proc R Soc Lond B Biol Sci 265: 1809–1817.

Puce A, Perrett D (2003) Electrophysiological and brain imaging of biological motion. Philosoph Trans Royal Soc Lond, Series B, 358: 435–445.

Ramachandran VS. Behavioral and magnetoencephalographic correlates of plasticity in the adult human brain. Proc Natl Acad Sci USA 1993; 90: 10413–20.

Ramachandran VS. Phantom limbs, neglect syndromes, repressed memories, and Freudian psychology. Int Rev Neurobiol 1994; 37: 291–333.

Ramachandran VS. Plasticity and functional recovery in neurology. Clin Med 2005; 5: 368–73.

Ramachandran VS, Hirstein W. The perception of phantom limbs. The D. O. Hebb lecture. Brain 1998; 121: 1603–30.

Ramachandran VS, Rogers-Ramachandran D, Cobb S. Touching the phantom limb. Nature 1995; 377: 489–90.

Ramachandran VS, Rogers-Ramachandran D. Phantom limbs and neural plasticity. Arch Neurol 2000; 57: 317–20.

Ramachandran VS, Rogers-Ramachandran D. It's all done with mirrors. Sci Am Mind 2007; 18: 16–9.

Ramachandran VS, Rogers-Ramachandran D. Sensations referred to a patient's phantom arm from another subjects intact arm: perceptual correlates of mirror neurons. Med Hypotheses 2008; 70: 1233–4.

Ramachandran VS, Rogers-Ramachandran D, Stewart M. Perceptual correlates of massive cortical reorganization. Science 1992; 258: 1159–60.

Rizzolatti G, Craighero L (2004) The mirror-neuron system. Annu Rev Neurosci 27: 169–192.

Rizzolatti G, Fogassi L, Gallese V (2001) Neurophysiological mechanisms underlying the understanding and imitation of action. Nature Rev Neurosci 2:661–670.

Rock I, Victor J. Vision and touch: an experimentally created conflict between the two senses. Science 1964; 143: 594–6.

Rose´n B, Lundborg G. Training with a mirror in rehabilitation of the hand. Scand J Plast Reconstr Surg Hand Surg 2005; 39: 104–8.

Royet JP, Plailly J, Delon-Martin C, Kareken DA, Segebarth C (2003) fMRI of emotional responses to odors: influence of hedonic valence and judgment, handedness, and gender. Neuroimage 20: 713–728.

Rozin R Haidt J and McCauley CR (2000) Disgust. In: Lewis M, Haviland-Jones JM (eds) Handbook of Emotion. 2nd Edition. Guilford Press, New York, pp 637–653.

Saxe R, Carey S, Kanwisher N (2004) Understanding other minds: linking developmental psychology and functional neuroimaging. Annu Rev Psychol 55: 87–124.

S. J. Russell and P. Norvig, Artificial intelligence: a modern approach (3rd edition): Prentice Hall, 2009.

Schienle A, Stark R, Walter B, Blecker C, Ott U, Kirsch P, Sammer G, Vaitl D (2002) The insula is not specifically involved in disgust processing: an fMRI study. Neuroreport 13: 2023–2026.

Showers MJC, Lauer EW (1961) Somatovisceral motor patterns in the insula. J Comp Neurol 117: 107–115.

Singer T, Seymour B, O'Doherty J, Kaube H, Dolan RJ, Frith CD (2004) Empathy for pain involves the affective but not the sensory components of pain. Science 303: 1157–1162.

Smith A (1759) The theory of moral sentiments (ed. 1976). Clarendon Press, Oxford.

S. N. Bose (1924). "Plancks Gesetz und Lichtquantenhypothese". Zeitschrift für Physik. 26 (1): 178–181.

Sprengelmeyer R, Rausch M, Eysel UT, Przuntek H (1998) Neural structures associated with recognition of facial expressions of basic emotions Proc R Soc Lond B Biol Sci 265: 1927–1931.

Strafella AP, Paus T (2000) Modulation of cortical excitability during action observation: a transcranial magnetic stimulation study. NeuroReport 11: 2289–2292.

Simonsen R (2015) Eating for the future: veganism and the challenge of in vitro meat. In: Stapleton P, Byers A (Hg). Biopolitics and utopia. Palgrave Macmillan, New York (2015), S 167–190

Tanaka K (1996) Inferotemporal cortex and object vision. Ann Rev Neurosci. 19: 109–140.

Tesla N. "My Inventions", 1919

T. R. Society, "Machine learning: the power and promise of computers that learn by example," ed. The Royal Society, 2017.

Tomasello M, Call J (1997) Primate cognition. Oxford University Press, Oxford.

Tremblay C, Robert M, Pascual-Leone A, Lepore F, Nguyen DK, Carmant L, Bouthillier A, Theoret H (2004) Action observation and execution: intracranial recordings in a human subject. Neurology. 63: 937–938.

Umilta MA, Kohler E, Gallese V, Fogassi L, Fadiga L, Keysers C, Rizzolatti G (2001) "I know what you are doing": a neurophysiological study. Neuron 32: 91–101.

Von Wright G.H., (1963), Norm and Action. A Logical Inquiry, Routledge & Kegan Paul, London.

Von Wright G.H., (1976), "Determinism and the Study of Man", in Essays on Explanation and Understanding, ed. by J. Manninen and R. Tuomela, Reidel, Dordrecht.

Von Wright G.H., (1977), "What is Humanism?", The Lindlay Lecture, University of Arkansas, Lawrence, Kansas.

Von Wright G.H., (1979), "Humanism and the Humanities", in Philosophy and Grammar, ed. by S. Kanger and S. Öhman, Reidel, Dordrecht, pp. 1-16. Reprinted in von Wright (1993).

Von Wright G.H., (1980), Freedom and Determination, North-Holland Publishing Co., Amsterdam.

Von Wright G.H., (1985), Of Human Freedom, The Tanner Lectures on Human Values,

Vol. VI, ed. by S. M. McMurrin, University of Utah Press, Salt Lake City, pp. 107-70. Reprinted in von Wright (1998).

Von Wright G.H., (1993), The Tree of Knowledge and Other Essays, Brill, Leiden.

Von Wright G.H., (1997), "Progress: Fact and Fiction", in The Idea of Progress, ed. by A. Burgen et al., W. de Gruyter, Berlin, pp. 1-18.

Von Wright G.H., (1998), In the Shadow of Descartes: Essays in the Philosophy of Mind, Kluwer, Dordrecht.

167

169

www.ingramcontent.com/pod-product-compliance
Lightning Source LLC
Chambersburg PA
CBHW051448250726
48655CB00001B/293

9 798670 557849